OUTSTANDING
LATERAL
THINKING
PUZZLES

OUTSTANDING
LATERAL
THINKING
PUZZLES

PAUL SLOANE & DES MacHALE

Illustrated by Steve Mack

STERLING PUBLISHING CO., INC.
NEW YORK

Edited by Jeanette Green
Designed by Kay Schuckhart
Illustrated by Steve Mack

Library of Congress Cataloging-in-Publication Data

Sloane, Paul, 1950–
   Outstanding lateral thinking puzzles / Paul Sloane & Des
MacHale ; illustrated by Steve Mack.
     p. cm.
   Includes index.
   ISBN-13: 978-1-4027-0380-5
   ISBN-10: 1-4027-0380-5
   1. Lateral thinking puzzles. I. MacHale, Des. II. Title.

GV1507.L37S5614 2005
793.73—dc22

2005013574

2 4 6 8 10 9 7 5 3

Published by Sterling Publishing Co., Inc.
387 Park Avenue South, New York, NY 10016
© 2005 by Paul Sloane and Des MacHale
Distributed in Canada by Sterling Publishing
c/o Canadian Manda Group, 165 Dufferin Street
Toronto, Ontario, Canada M6K 3H6
Distributed in Great Britain and Europe by Chris Lloyd at Orca Book
Services, Stanley House, Fleets Lane, Poole BH15 3AJ, England
Distributed in Australia by Capricorn Link (Australia) Pty. Ltd.
P.O. Box 704, Windsor, NSW 2756, Australia

Sterling ISBN 1-4027-0380-5

For information about custom editions, special sales, premium and
corporate purchases, please contact Sterling Special Sales
Department at 800-805-5489 or specialsales@sterlingpub.com.

ACKNOWLEDGMENTS

We thank Jason Burge for "Quarters," João Gonçalves for "Oskar," Torgeir Apeland for "A Difference in Attitude," Kate Fallon for "Bump," Micheal O'Fiachra for "Racing Certainty," Andrew Katz for "Cheaper by the Dozen," Brian Hobbs for "Death by Reading," Lynne Payne for "Elementary," David Burn for "Deadly Talk" and "Second of One," and Felicia Ackerman for "The Fruit of Sarcasm."

CONTENTS

Introduction 9

Puzzles 11

WALLY Test I 29

Clues 49

WALLY Test II 68

Puzzle Answers 69

WALLY Test I Answers 91

WALLY Test II Answers 92

Index 93

INTRODUCTION

"All men are mortal. Socrates is a man. Therefore, Socrates is mortal." So runs classical logic as it's popularly taught in schools and colleges. Of course, the trouble is that real-life situations are rarely that simple or straightforward. The types of logic and deduction we all use in everyday thinking are much more likely to be an unpredictable mixture of guesswork, hunches, funny feelings, insight, intuition, experience, sixth sense, serendipity, low cunning, street wisdom, and a whole host of other delightful techniques, some of which don't even have names. Luckily, these techniques can be used by all people who enjoy exercising their minds. However, one of the most powerful weapons the human mind can employ does have a name. We call it *lateral thinking*.

Now, lateral thinking has been around as long as people have been, but it's only recently that we've become more attuned to it. Lateral thinking involves "sideways" thinking, nonlinear thinking, asking "What if?" and lots of other questions that may appear quite silly at first hearing. The first person to build an irrigation canal, vital for human survival in some parts of the world, was a lateral thinker: "Rain is not falling on my crops to water them, but rain is falling on places some distance away. Why not build a canal and let gravity carry the water from where it is not needed to where it is wanted?" Most inventors, innovators, and engineers are lateral thinkers, as are many clever lawyers and successful businesspeople. Whatever you work at, there is a huge potential for lateral thinking in your life and work, if only you can find out how to implement it.

Well, one way to kick-start this delightful process is to practice lateral thinking by solving the lateral-thinking puzzles we've assembled for you in this book and in other books in this series. Here's how you play the game: Take one of the scenarios listed here, and with the help of a question master who knows the solution, pose a series of questions with a yes or no answer until you unravel the solution. If you get stuck (and we all do from time to time), there are clues to help you along, until you come to that glorious moment when you complete the circuit in your brain and the solution suddenly emerges. (Aha!)

The process can be enormously enjoyable for both individuals and groups, in the classroom, on car or train journeys, or even during a quick coffee break. In no time at all you'll become an accomplished lateral thinker, learning to ask questions so obvious you would never have thought of asking them previously and challenging assumptions you were not even aware you had made. This is the first step in learning to use the hidden lateral part of your mind that's just bursting to be unleashed. Have fun!

PUZZLES

Quarters

A man and his wife are dead. If the man had had just one quarter, his wife would have lived. If he had had two quarters, he would have lived. If he had had three quarters, both the man and his wife would have lived, but his brother would have died. Why?

Find clues on p. 50 and the answer on p. 70.

Oskar

Oskar Kokoschka, an Austrian abstract expressionist painter, arrived in England in 1938, after having escaped from the Nazi terror in Europe. Kokoschka was an artist and had never been a politician, yet he blamed himself for the dangerous state that Europe was in, and later for the catastrophe of World War II. Why?

Find clues on p. 50 and the answer on p. 70.

Drink and Die I

On a very dark night, a man was outside walking. When he came around a corner, he saw a building on which were written the words "Drink and Die." What did it mean?

Find clues on p. 50 and the answer on p. 70.

Drink and Die II

Two men wearing helmets drank some cool beer and then died. If they had drunk warm beer, they would have lived. What happened?

Find clues on p. 50 and the answer on p. 70.

13

Traffic Offense

A man goes to work in the same manner every working day for twenty years. However, one morning going to work in the same way, he is arrested by the police. Why?

Find clues on p. 50 and the answer on p. 71.

Bad Bump

Julie bumped into George and they both died. Why?

Find clues on p. 51 and the answer on p. 71.

The Clever Detective

When the detective arrived at the scene of the crime, he had no idea who the criminal was. He turned to his assistant and said: "We are looking for someone with the initials A and S." How did he know?

Find clues on p. 51 and the answer on p. 71.

The Silent Robber

The manager of a factory was very concerned to learn that valuable copper had gone missing again during the night. The security guards assured him that the security was very tight and no one could have gotten in or out of the factory. What was happening?

Find clues on p. 51 and the answer on p. 72.

A Difference in Attitude

The driver of an underground train made an announcement that infuriated some of his passengers and amused the other passengers. What was it?

Find clues on p. 51 and the answer on p. 72.

Insecure

A new, seemingly superior security device for houses is marketed. However, in practice, it turns out to be inferior to existing, conventional systems. Why?

Find clues on p. 52 and the answer on p. 72.

Deadly Talk

The speech killed the President. How come?

Find clues on p. 52 and the answer on p. 72.

The Fruit of Sarcasm

What he had intended to be a sarcastic statement resulted in an invention that's now in common use. What is it?

Find clues on p. 52 and the answer on p. 73.

Timepiece

Why are most watches shown in magazines fixed at the time ten to two or ten past ten?

Find clues on p. 52 and the answer on p. 73.

Racing Certainty

In an international 100-meter sprint race, the athlete who ran the 100 meters in the fastest time was not the winner of the race. Why?

Find clues on p. 52 and the answer on p. 73.

No Claims Bonus

A stuntman has to insure himself every time he jumps from a height. He does this and performs the jump, but something goes wrong and he is crippled for life. The insurance company refuses to pay out. Why?

Find clues on p. 53 and the answer on p. 73.

Second of One

They had no one to beat but came in second. How come?

Find clues on p. 53 and the answer on p. 74.

Death by Reading

She died because she was a voracious reader. How come?

Find clues on p. 53 and the answer on p. 74.

My Condiments to the Chef

It is possible to buy wine flavored with salt and pepper to use in cooking. But since you can always add salt and pepper to table wine, why does anybody bother to produce cooking wine?

Find clues on p. 53 and the answer on p. 74.

Elementary

··

When she saw the fishing boat in the far distance, she knew that it had already hauled in its catch. How did she know?

Find clues on p. 54 and the answer on p. 74.

Taking the Right Steps

··

Two men carried a ladder that was 18 feet (5.4 m) long down a corridor in a hotel. The corridor was 8 feet (2.4 m) high and 6 feet (1.8 m) wide. They came to a T-shape junction with another corridor of the same dimensions in the same building. There were no windows or doors they could use, and the ladder was one single piece with no joints. How did they get the ladder around the bend?

Find clues on p. 54 and the answer on p. 74.

Only in the U.S.A.

On the fourteenth of March each year in the United States, there is a certain celebration that does not take place in Europe. In fact, this celebration would never take place in Europe. Why?

Find clues on p. 54 and the answer on p. 75.

Cheaper by the Dozen

The more gas I use, the lower the bill from my gas supplier. Why?

Find clues on p. 55 and the answer on p. 75.

Lakeless

A man in the woods came to a place where he knew a small lake had been. When he found that the lake was not there, he knew that he was in mortal danger. Why?

Find clues on p. 55 and the answer on p. 76.

Red-Faced

A man who received a signed copy of a book in the mail was severely embarrassed. Why?

Find clues on p. 55 and the answer on p. 76.

Picture Book

Why did this weatherman draw a little picture of a ship on a map of the Atlantic Ocean?

Find clues on p. 55 and the answer on p. 76.

Poor Pet

Despite the fact that it involved the unfortunate death of an animal, it was hailed as one of the greatest human achievements of all time. What was it?

Find clues on p. 56 and the answer on p. 76.

High Flyer

A man who was boarding a plane was severely embarrassed when the airplane's engines started. Why?

Find clues on p. 56 and the answer on p. 76.

Birds of a Feather

Why does a flock of birds fly in a V-shape formation?

Find clues on p. 56 and the answer on p. 77.

Deadly Delivery

A man was killed, and as a result, the post office has had to deliver millions more pieces of mail. Who was he?

Find clues on p. 56 and the answer on p. 77.

Fatal Fork

A man went to work carrying a fork and a net. Another man died. How?

Find clues on p. 56 and the answer on p. 77.

Groovy Movie

A famous director came to Ireland to make a film. Many local people thought that they would be able to get jobs as extras. They were surprised at the criteria the director had for selecting local extras. What was he looking for?

Find clues on p. 57 and the answer on p. 77.

Double Your Money

Why does a man cut all his banknotes in two?

Find clues on p. 57 and the answer on p. 78.

Malfunction

A man had a piece of machinery that was not working. So he opened it up and discovered a 2-inch (5-cm) moth flying around inside the machine. He took the moth out, cleaned the machine, and found that it worked very well. His actions have given us a useful new phrase in the modern English language. What is the phrase?

Find clues on p. 57 and the answer on p. 78.

A Friendly Match?

After a friendly football game, the two teams shook hands and then tried to kill each other. Why?

Find clues on p. 57 and the answer on p. 78.

Lifesaver

A man held a newspaper very close to his chest in order to save his life. How?

Find clues on p. 57 and the answer on p. 79.

The Plant

Why does a policeman put a plastic bag of talcum powder in a woman's coat pocket?

Find clues on p. 58 and the answer on p. 79.

Insert Memory Here

Memory Transplant

A man was so forgetful that he needed an operation. What was it for?

Find clues on p. 58 and the answer on p. 79.

The Moggy's Ming

Why does a man feed his cat using a very valuable Ming bowl?

Find clues on p. 58 and the answer on p. 79.

Stranger Danger

A stranger came to the house. No one had seen him before. He stayed just one week, did not say a word, and then left. Everyone was sad when he went. Who was he?

Find clues on p. 58 and the answer on p. 80.

WALLY Test I

1. What kind of men can never die of old age?

2. What three-letter word completes the first word and starts the second?
   DON   CAR

3. A man owed a huge amount of money. He paid half of it. How much does he owe now?

4. What sort of fur do you get from a tiger?

5. Where are the Pyrenees?

6. Who was the tallest president of the United States?

7. What does a duck do if it flies upside down?

8. Why was the postman unlucky?

9. Who are the most dependable staff in a hospital?

Find the answers on p. 91.

The Lethal Lie

A man was captured and interrogated. His captors tell him, truthfully, that if he answers their questions truthfully, his life will be spared. Although he answers their questions truthfully, they immediately shoot him dead. Why?

Find clues on p. 59 and the answer on p. 80.

Focus Pocus

A very precious jewel is on display at an exhibition. A guard is hired to protect it for an hour and promises not to take his eyes off it for that period. However, at the end of the hour, the jewel is examined and found to be a fake. At the beginning of the hour, it was genuine. The guard swears that he never took his eyes off the jewel during the hour, and he is an honest man. What had happened?

Find clues on p. 59 and the answer on p. 80.

Outrage

....

Who were the first couple to appear on prime-time television in bed together?

Find clues on p. 59 and the answer on p. 80.

First Time, Last Time

....

A dancer performed a dance in front of a large audience. It was a dance he had never rehearsed. What was going on?

Find clues on p. 59 and the answer on p. 81.

Speechless

....

Pierre was a healthy young man. He had not seen his friends or family for a while. Then something happened. When he saw his friends and family, he could not speak to them. Why?

Find clues on p. 59 and the answer on p. 81.

Meeting and Greeting

....

A woman was hurrying down a street when she met an old friend she had not seen for many years. She did not shake hands or wave to her friend. Why not?

Find clues on p. 60 and the answer on p. 81.

Playacting

A rich man wrote a bad play and paid a producer a lot of money in return for his promise to put it on stage for him as part of a theatrical evening. The producer did this, but when the playwright attended the opening performance, he was very angry. Why?

Find clues on p. 60 and the answer on p. 81.

The Uneaten

A little boy and girl were thrilled when their father gave them Easter eggs. But they never ate them—why not?

Find clues on p. 60 and the answer on p. 81.

Walk of Death

A woman went out for a walk on a summer's day. She was later found dead with severe head injuries. The police fail to find any murder weapon. How did she die?

Find clues on p. 60 and the answer on p. 82.

Defensive Measure

Security firms used to advise clients who wanted to protect their houses to build high walls around them to keep out burglars and other intruders. Now they simply recommend fences. The walls and fences were equally difficult to scale. So why switch to fences?

Find clues on p. 61 and the answer on p. 82.

Shaping the World

Why did a former world leader copyright a strange shape?

Find clues on p. 61 and the answer on p. 82.

The Shot That Saved

A woman took a photo of her son that saved his life. How?

Find clues on p. 61 and the answer on p. 82.

False Confession

Why did a man call the police and tell them that he had shot someone when he had not?

Find clues on p. 61 and the answer on p. 83.

Garment for Rent

Why did a man destroy the sweater that his wife had made for him?

Find clues on p. 61 and the answer on p. 83.

Key Decision

A man wishes to enter a building, so he acquires a key to the front door of the building. It is the correct key that fits and would indeed open the lock. However, when he tries to enter the building, he finds that he cannot. There is no other person or guard dog around, and no other lock, bolt, or restraint on the door. Why can he not gain entry to the building?

Find clues on p. 62 and the answer on p. 84.

A Long Way to Go for a Drink

A man travels to another country in order to have a drink in a bar. He could have had the same drink in a bar in his home country. Why did he travel?

Find clues on p. 62 and the answer on p. 84.

Pop the Question

A man proposed to a woman. She promised she would give him her answer at dinner the following week. After they had dinner, she said, "Do you want my answer?" He replied, "I know it already." How did he know?

Find clues on p. 62 and the answer on p. 84.

Custom and Practice

Mark Twain was stopped by Customs and asked what he had in his suitcase. He replied, "Just clothes." However, when the official searched his suitcase, he found a large bottle of whisky on which Twain would have to pay duty. What explanation did Twain give that caused the official to smile and let him through without payment?

Find clues on p. 62 and the answer on p. 84.

Towitt, Towoo

A man walking through a small forest finds a stuffed owl perched on a branch of a tree. Why is the stuffed owl there?

Find clues on p. 63 and the answer on p. 84.

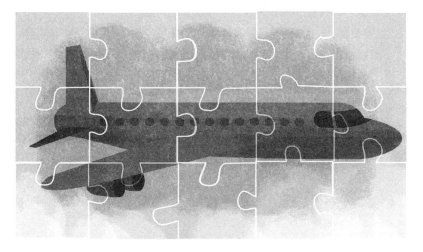

Plane Puzzler

. . . .

A plane flying at 25,000 feet (7,500 meters) suddenly switches off all its engines but is in no danger. Why?

Find clues on p. 63 and the answer on p. 85.

High Caliber

. . . .

A man was shot many times and lived. His wife was shot just once and died. How come?

Find clues on p. 63 and the answer on p. 85.

Wounded Enemy

. . . .

A man shoots his enemy and wounds him severely, but he's careful not to kill him. Why?

Find clues on p. 63 and the answer on p. 85.

Smoking Is Bad for You

A man comes home and finds his wife smoking a cigarette. No word is exchanged between them. The man goes over to a broom closet, hauls another man out of it, and flattens him with a punch. The husband and wife smile and embrace each other. What is going on?

Find clues on p. 64 and the answer on p. 85.

Determined to Die

Jacques was determined to commit suicide. He stood on top of a seaside cliff and tied a noose around his neck and tied the other end of the rope to a large rock. Then Jacques drank poison and set fire to his clothes. He had a gun ready to shoot himself. He jumped from the cliff and fired the pistol. What happened?

Find clues on p. 64 and the answer on p. 86.

Hello, Grandma!

When her grandmother dropped in to visit her at her office, a woman was severely embarrassed. Why?

Find clues on p. 64 and the answer on p. 86.

Cake Killer

A woman ate a slice of cake with her fingers. Afterwards she did not wash her hands. As a result of this, she died a few hours later. Why?

Find clues on p. 64 and the answer on p. 87.

41

Vacation, Vacation, Vacation

Why does a major bank insist that all its employees take two weeks' vacation in one stretch? It has nothing to do with the welfare of the employees.

Find clues on p. 64 and the answer on p. 87.

Clerical Advantage

Bishops could have seven. Priests could have five. Ordinary people could only have one. What is it?

Find clues on p. 65 and the answer on p. 87.

Bad Loser

A man playing in the final round of a tough competition loses. In a fit of anger, he shoots the winner with a gun with the result that his opponent can never play again. However, the police are not called, and the man escapes with a fine and a simple warning. Why?

Find clues on p. 65 and the answer on p. 87.

Puppy Love

Children got into trouble because of a dog, which was well trained and very well behaved.

Find clues on p. 65 and the answer on p. 88.

Death at the Door

A woman dialed 911 to ask for help. She was told not to open her door but to open her window. She first tried to open the window, and then the door. She died. Why?

Find clues on p. 65 and the answer on p. 88.

The Lethal Warning

A man died because he warned his friend of danger. How?

Find clues on p. 66 and the answer on p. 88.

Field of Gold

Why did a farmer spray his field with golden dye?

Find clues on p. 66 and the answer on p. 88.

Good Bump

A woman driver usually slowed down when approaching a speed bump in the road, but one day she accelerated toward one and drove over it quite quickly. Why?

Find clues on p. 66 and the answer on p. 88.

Timeless

Which woman has appeared most often on the cover of *Time* magazine?

Find clues on p. 66 and the answer on p. 89.

Chilly

What desert is the coldest on Earth and why?

Find clues on p. 66 and the answer on p. 89.

The Silly Salesman

A salesman died because he was preparing for his sales call. How?

Find clues on p. 67 and the answer on p. 89.

It's Not True!

Why did the teacher write this on the blackboard: "Woman without her man is helpless"?

Find clues on p. 67 and the answer on p. 89.

Not Here, Son

A schoolboy was an avid athlete. The police in the village where he lived stopped him from practicing athletic feats. Why?

Find clues on p. 67 and the answer on p. 89.

Unsanitary Janitor

Why did the janitor dip his mop in the toilet before cleaning the bathroom mirror?

Find clues on p. 67 and the answer on p. 90.

Hyper-Inflation

Why did a bottle of wine jump in value a thousandfold overnight?

Find clues on p. 67 and the answer on p. 90.

CLUES

Quarters

* The quarters he needed were coins.
* He had discovered that his brother intended to kill him and his wife.
* He drove to a gas station.
* He had a medical condition.

Oskar

* Kokoschka had fought for Germany in World War I, but he was not a military man and hated war.
* He had applied to study art at the academy and had succeeded in gaining entry.
* He never met Hitler.

Drink and Die I

* The sign was on a restaurant.
* There was no evil intent.
* Something was not working.

Drink and Die II

* They did not get drunk. No vehicles were involved.
* They slowly drank some beer and suffocated to death.
* They had wanted to keep their beer very cold.

Traffic Offense

* He drives to work.
* Something had changed, but it was more fundamental than just a traffic light.
* How had he forgotten after all that publicity?

Bad Bump

* Julie and George were a woman and a man who had not met before, and they did not speak when they bumped into each other.

* Julie did not hurt George when she bumped into him, but shortly afterward they were both killed by a massive blow.

* Both were traveling, but not on any vehicle.

The Clever Detective

* The crime was a robbery.

* It took place at a border crossing.

* The detective saw what was missing.

The Silent Robber

* The security was very tight with alarms, lights, and guard dogs to deter and detect intruders.

* The copper that was taken was in the form of balls of wire.

* The copper was being systematically removed, but not by a criminal.

A Difference in Attitude

* He made two announcements; the first was a warning.

* Some passengers got off the train.

* The honest passengers laughed when they heard his second announcement.

Insecure

* The new security device was designed to deter burglars, but in some ways it helped them.
* The new device involved very strong lights that lit up certain areas brilliantly.
* The strong lights also produced something else.

Deadly Talk

* The President of the United States was killed as an indirect result of a speech he made.
* He was not assassinated. He died accidentally.
* The speech was his inauguration speech.
* It was given in Washington in March 1841.

The Fruit of Sarcasm

* A chef was displeased with the comments of a customer.
* He deliberately exaggerated certain aspects of the dish he prepared.
* It is now a very popular snack.

Timepiece

* Advertising agencies prefer a personal, positive, and friendly image. How does ten to two help this?

Racing Certainty

* This was a regular 100-meter race run by normal athletes competing to win.
* The man who ran the fastest 100 meters crossed the line second.
* All competitors were in the blocks at the same time and heard the starter's gun.

No Claims Bonus

* He did not try to defraud or cheat the insurance company.

* The nature of his accident is not relevant. The insurance company refused on a technical issue.

* The stuntman took great care to prepare for the jump. He measured the tower carefully, well in advance.

* Something changed about the tower.

Second of One

* This involves a team in a competition.

* They were the only contestants.

* They were awarded second place.

Death by Reading

* She read books and magazines.

* The topic of her reading is not relevant.

* She was murdered by her husband.

* She was poisoned.

My Condiments to the Chef

* There is no financial or tax advantage in producing or buying cooking wine.

* The benefit relates to the fact that the wine can only used for cooking.

* Restaurant owners prefer to use cooking wine because it reduces a risk.

Elementary

* This does not have to do with the weight of the boat. It is not possible to see if it is lower in the water.

* It does not involve the direction of the boat or anything happening on shore.

* This does not involve the fishing gear, the crew, or any signal from the boat.

* The fishermen first haul in the nets and then process the fish.

* They dispose of scraps they do not want.

Taking the Right Steps

* The men carried the ladder around the corner very easily.

* No mathematics or calculations are needed for the solution.

* Check your assumptions on this ladder.

Only in the U.S.A.

* The day is not named after a person, and no celebrity is involved in the day.

* The day does not commemorate any historical event or anything to do with the origin, politics, or history of the United States.

* The way the Americans write the date is relevant.

* Mathematicians celebrate this day.

Cheaper by the Dozen

* Under certain circumstances, I can reduce the bill from the energy company by using more gas.

* The gas is used to heat my house and water.

* The price of the gas per cubic foot does not become lower as more gas is used.

* Gas is one of the most efficient fuels for heating.

Lakeless

* The man was in danger but not from an animal or a person.

* The lake had evaporated, but the weather was not a factor.

* There was a natural catastrophe.

Red-Faced

* He knew the author.

* The subject of the book is not relevant. It was not undesirable in any way.

* The author had written a dedication in the book.

Picture Book

* This has nothing to do with the weather.

* This does not have to do with boats, but has to do with transport.

* The man was sending a signal.

Poor Pet

* A dog was sent on a journey which it did not survive.

* There was enormous political interest in this experiment.

High Flyer

* He was a passenger who caught the right plane at the right time for his destination.

* It was a normal flight, and the flight went smoothly.

* If he had been on board the plane when the engines started, then he would not have been embarrassed.

Birds of a Feather

* There are thought to be two main benefits to the birds. One has to do with energy.

* Why not fly in a long line?

Deadly Delivery

* The man had nothing to do with the mail or post office.

* The extra mail was not informing people about the man or his death.

* He was a good person but not especially important in his day.

Fatal Fork

* The first man killed the second man.

* They had not known each other before this day.

* The killing was not accidental.

* Many people witnessed the event, but the man was not charged with murder or any other crime.

Groovy Movie

* The director was making a film about World War II.

* He wanted extras for the battle scenes.

* The movie was *Saving Private Ryan*.

Double Your Money

* He does it for security.

* He intends that the notes be put back together.

Malfunction

* The piece of machinery was high technology.

* The expression refers to a fault or malfunction.

A Friendly Match?

* They were not professional or even regular football players.

* They were not criminals, but they were enemies.

* This happened in France.

Lifesaver

* The newspaper did not directly protect him from a weapon or from danger.

* It did not staunch a wound.

* It was that same day's newspaper, and it served as information that helped save him.

The Plant

* The policeman was not trying to frame or incriminate the woman. He was trying to find out the truth.
* The woman did not know the bag was there until she was told about it.
* The bag looked as though it might be drugs.
* This was not a training exercise.

Memory Transplant

* The operation was not a transplant or a brain operation.
* He tended to forget where he put things.
* He still forgot things after the operation; however, it meant that he had one less thing to worry about.

The Moggy's Ming

* The cat and its food are not important.
* He is aware that the bowl is very valuable.
* He hopes that people will notice, but he's not trying to impress them.
* He does it for financial gain.

Stranger Danger

* The stranger was a human.
* They were expecting him.
* He did not perform a service for them.
* Although he did not say a word, he did utter some sounds.

The Lethal Lie

* Criminals who wanted to know where some money was hidden interrogated the man.
* He answered truthfully and told where the money was.
* The criminals and the man were deceived.
* There was a language issue.

Focus Pocus

* For the hour, the guard pointed his head toward the gem and kept looking at it.
* The clever thief managed to switch the gem even while the guard thought he was looking at it.
* No visual trickery or mirrors were involved.
* The thief got the guard to close his eyes momentarily.

Outrage

* They were husband and wife.
* No one, not even the most sensitive, was offended.

First Time, Last Time

* This historical event was not a dance as such.
* He did not do it to entertain the audience. He did not want to do it.
* The dancer's body performed powerful and involuntary gyrations.

Speechless

* Pierre was punished.
* He saw the people momentarily.
* He had been held in prison.

Meeting and Greeting

* The woman would normally have shaken hands with her friend, but today she was not able to.
* She was rushing today, but her hurry was not the only reason that she did not shake hands with her friend.
* She was rushing to the hospital.
* She had suffered a serious accident.

Playacting

* The play that the rich man saw was well produced and well acted.
* The producer kept his word to the man, but not in the way that the man had expected.
* The play the man wrote appeared on the stage.

The Uneaten

* The boy and girl were healthy and enjoyed chocolate.
* The eggs were unusual.
* They were a royal family.

Walk of Death

* She was not murdered.
* She was killed in a freak accident.
* Heavy blows killed her where she was found.
* No one removed the items that killed her, but nothing was found.

Defensive Measure
* It was found that fences provided better security than walls.
* More burglars were caught and more were deterred.
* Fences have gaps.

Shaping the World
* The shape was personal to him.
* He copyrighted it to protect his personal image.
* He was Russian.

The Shot That Saved
* The photo revealed a life-threatening condition.
* The photograph was of the boy's face.
* She used flash photography.

False Confession
* The man had not shot anyone, and he had not committed a crime other than misleading the police.
* He was frustrated with the police.
* He wanted the police to apprehend some criminals.

Garment for Rent
* By destroying the sweater, he saved his life.
* The sweater was never a danger to him.
* He put the sweater to another use.

Key Decision

* This is not a normal building.

* The door can be opened with this key, but the man cannot open the door.

* A security feature prevents him from opening the door.

A Long Way to Go for a Drink

* The man was not going on vacation. There was no other reason for his trip than to visit a bar.

* He did not meet anyone.

* Any bar would do after he reached his destination.

* Drinking was not his only vice.

Pop the Question

* The woman was not wearing anything that would give an indication of her decision.

* The man deduced that she would refuse his offer of marriage.

* It was related to what she ate.

Custom and Practice

* Mark Twain cleverly described the drink.

* He justified it as an article of clothing.

* What could he have called it?

Towitt, Towoo

* Someone deliberately placed the stuffed owl in the tree.
* The owl was not there to advise people about hunting. It also wasn't intended to deter or warn other creatures or people.
* A shopkeeper put it there to aid business.
* The owl did not carry any signage or advertising.

Plane Puzzler

* All the plane's engines were turned off, and they closed down.
* The plane did not glide or use a balloon, parachute, or lighter-than-air gases.
* The plane continued to fly but not under its own power.

High Caliber

* The man did not wear any protective clothing.
* A gun was involved but no bullets.
* They were entertainers.

Wounded Enemy

* He did not act out of kindness or mercy.
* The men were deadly enemies in opposing armed forces.
* Winning the war was more important than killing every enemy.

Smoking Is Bad for You

* The husband acted to protect himself and his wife.

* The man in the broom closet was a threat to the man and woman.

* The wife did not normally smoke.

Determined to Die

* Jacques died, but not from a gunshot.

* He also did not die from hanging or poison.

* He did not die from the fire.

Hello, Grandma!

* The grandmother was as normal as a grandmother can be.

* The grandmother did not do, say, or wear anything embarrassing.

* The presence of the grandmother demonstrated a deceit.

Cake Killer

* There was nothing poisonous or unhygienic about the cake, the plate, or her hands.

* It was a sugary cake, and some of the sugar stayed on her hands.

* She had a medical condition.

Vacation, Vacation, Vacation

* The bank is acting out of self-interest.

* There are financial benefits to the bank for the two-week break, but it has nothing to do with vacation pay or employee benefits.

* The bank is concerned about fraud.

Clerical Advantage

* It is something religious.

* It is not a title, name, rite, or costume.

* It is not used while you are alive.

Bad Loser

* The loser used a real gun with real bullets with the intention of harming his opponent.

* The man and his opponent were competing against each other to win the prize.

* The man was playing a board game.

Puppy Love

* The dog did something that showed that the children were misbehaving.

* The children were at school.

* The dog did something that it had been trained to do.

* The dog did not belong to a teacher, and it did not belong to any of the children.

Death at the Door

* The woman was not under attack.

* She was not at home or at work.

* There was in no danger from fire.

* The door and window would normally open correctly. However, she was unable to open either of them because of the situation in which she found herself.

The Lethal Warning

* His warning caused the very danger he feared.

* He was killed in an accident.

* His friend heard his warning.

* No one else was involved.

Field of Gold

* The golden dye did not serve any agricultural purpose.

* Someone asked him to change the appearance of the field.

* It was for an artistic purpose.

Good Bump

* It was her car, and she was not trying to damage it.

* She was not in danger.

* She had forgotten something.

Timeless

* This woman is not a film star, actress, television personality, politician, or pop star.

Chilly

* A desert is defined as a place with very little or no precipitation.

The Silly Salesman

* The salesman was not testing a product.

* He did not sell dangerous products.

* He drove to his appointment.

* He died in a car accident.

It's Not True!

* She was an English teacher.

* She was teaching the value of correct punctuation.

Not Here, Son

* The boy wanted to practice a particular athletic event.

* He was a runner.

* People considered what he did disrespectful.

Unsanitary Janitor

* The janitor was following instructions.

* Although what he did was unhygienic, he did it with worthy motives.

* He worked at a school.

* His action was designed to improve behavior.

Hyper-Inflation

* It was not a particularly rare or unusual vintage of wine.

* The bottle became valuable as a collector's item.

* This involves some celebrities.

WALLY Test II

1. How can a boy switch off the light that's 10 feet (about 3 meters) from his bed and get into bed before it is dark?

2. You're standing in line at the ticket desk at an airport. The man in front of you is going to New York. The woman behind you is going to London. Where are you going?

3. Who are always after you?

4. If a cat can kill a rat in two minutes, how long would it take a cat to kill 100 rats?

5. What can move and be still at the same time?

6. Why does a postman call his bag John and not Jane?

7. What kind of rocks are found just below the surface of Lake Superior?

8. February is the shortest month; what is the longest month?

9. Where are the best parties on a cruise ship?

Find the answers on p. 92.

PUZZLE
ANSWERS

Quarters

The man has learned that his brother planned to kill him and his wife in order to take over the family business. The man was driving through the desert to warn his wife that his brother was going to kill her. He intended to kill his brother, but he was diabetic and had to stop for sugar. He reached a gas station, but it was closed and he had no change. He could not make the phone call to save his wife (one quarter). He could not get something sweet from the vending machine (two quarters). Hence he died and his brother killed his wife.

Oskar

Oskar Kokoschka (1886–1980) applied to study at the Academy of Arts in Vienna in 1907. A young man called Adolf Hitler also applied. Oskar was successful but Hitler just missed being accepted. Had Hitler taken Oskar's place, it is likely he would have followed art rather than politics as a career.

Drink and Die I

It was a restaurant that had a neon sign that said "Drink and Dine." Unfortunately, the light in the third letter N had failed.

Drink and Die II

They went caving and took some beers with them in a cooler (cool box) packed with dry ice to keep the beer cold. They opened the box. The dry ice melted and formed carbon dioxide. Because carbon dioxide is denser than air, it drove the oxygen out of the small, low cave. They suffocated to death.

Traffic Offense

The man was a Swedish motorist who drove to work on the left side of the road as he had for the previous twenty years. Unfortunately for him, it was on the day that Sweden changed over to driving on the right-hand side of the road.

Bad Bump

Julie and George were both skydivers. George had his parachute deployed when Julie crashed into it. It collapsed around her, thus preventing her from opening her parachute.

The Clever Detective

A thief had stolen two letters from the sign at the border that said "Welcome to the USA." Now it said "Welcome to the U."

The Silent Robber

The security guards had a German Shepherd, that roamed the factory. It took the bright balls of copper and buried them in the factory yard.

A Difference in Attitude

As the train pulled into the station, the driver announced over the public-address system: "There will be a team of ticket inspectors entering at the next station, so those without a valid ticket may want to leave here." Many people left the train. As the driver closed the doors and set the train in motion again, he announced through the external speakers: "I was just joking."

Insecure

The security device cast much brighter lights outside dwellings. Brighter lights cast more intense shadows, which burglars used for better hiding places.

Deadly Talk

William Henry Harrison (1773–1841) was the ninth president of the United States and the first to die in office. He gave an inaugural speech in the cold Washington drizzle in March 1841. The speech lasted 100 minutes and he did not wear a hat or coat. He contracted pneumonia and died a month later.

The Fruit of Sarcasm

In a restaurant, the chef was annoyed by a customer who kept sending back his French fries, complaining that they were too thick and not crispy enough. So the chef cut the potatoes as thinly as he possibly could, and fried them so that they were as crisp as possible. These became the potato chips we know today.

Timepiece

The idea seems to have come from Japan, and the configuration looks like a happy, smiling face.

Racing Certainty

This is supposed to have happened to Carl Lewis. Although he ran the 100 meters faster than anyone else, his starting reaction time was slow. This meant that he did not start until 0.05 seconds had elapsed. The race was won by somebody who started after 0.03 seconds, and although Lewis ran the 100 meters faster than the winner, he came in second.

No Claims Bonus

The stuntman insures himself to jump off a tower that is 300 meters tall. He measures it in winter and insures himself to jump from that height. But the jump takes place in summer when, due to expansion of the metal, the tower is several centimeters (a few inches) taller. The insurance company refuses to pay his injury claim.

Second of One

In Arklow, Ireland, in the County of Wicklow, an annual music festival is held. In the contest for choirs in 1978, there was only one entrant. The Dublin Welsh Male Voice Choir, despite being the only contender in a field of one, managed to come in second. Because they had arrived an hour late, the judges did not award them first prize.

Death by Reading

While on a business trip, a man sends his wife a magazine. Aware of her habit of licking her finger before turning each page, he puts poison on the corners of several pages. The poison transfers from page to finger to mouth, thus killing her.

My Condiments to the Chef

Wine flavored with salt and pepper is sold to hotels and restaurants for use in cooking. They do not want to buy ordinary wine because they fear that kitchen staff will drink it.

Elementary

She saw a flock of seagulls following the boat. Seagulls prefer that someone else does the fishing so that they can easily collect the scraps. Fishermen throw scraps from their haul overboard.

Taking the Right Steps

They were carrying a rope ladder.

Only in the U.S.A

On March 14th every year in the United States, some people celebrate Pi = 3.14 day, which is not a possible date on the European calendar. (In Europe, when dates are given, the day always precedes the month: 14.3.)

Cheaper by the Dozen

My energy company supplies both gas and electricity. I get one bill for both. I previously used the electric immersion heater to provide my hot water. When I turned the gas thermostat up, I used a lot more gas but no electricity for heating water. Using gas to heat water is a lot cheaper than electricity, hence the reduction in the bill.

Lakeless

A volcano had erupted nearby. When the man reached the site of the lake, the molten lava had reached the other side and caused the lake to evaporate. He knew that it would now reach him soon.

Red-Faced

George Bernard Shaw was browsing in a second-hand bookshop one day when he found a book he had signed, "With compliments, George Bernard Shaw," and given to a friend. The friend had sold it to the shop. Shaw bought the book and inscribed it, "With renewed compliments, George Bernard Shaw," and sent it again to the friend. The friend was mortified.

Picture Book

The man who drew a ship on the map of the Atlantic Ocean was a television weather forecaster who was sending a message to his wife to pick him up after work because he had no other means of transport. This happened in the early days of the Irish television weather service before cell (mobile) phones.

Poor Pet

The first artificial earth satellite was launched by the Soviet Union in 1957. The cosmonaut called Laika died in the experiment because he was unable to withstand the temperature and pressure. Laika was a dog.

High Flyer

As he walked toward the aircraft, its engines started and his wig was blown off.

Birds of a Feather

It reduces air resistance on the flock, and each bird has a clear view of what's in front. As with Olympic indoor cyclists, each bird takes a turn doing the more demanding front-flying task.

Deadly Delivery

The man was a Christian martyr called Valentine, whose feastday was declared by the pope in the fifth century. Valentine's Day on February 14 celebrates his memory. Nowadays it is the signal for millions of valentine cards to be sent. According to estimates, one billion valentine cards are sent each year, second only to Christmas cards.

Fatal Fork

The man was a gladiator in ancient Rome. His weapons were a trident (a fork-shaped spear) and a net. His task was to fight another man to the death for the entertainment of the crowd.

Groovy Movie

Director Steven Spielberg came to Ireland to film Saving Private Ryan. He needed extras for the D-Day landing scenes. His particular need was for people who had only one leg or one arm. They were made up to look like able-bodied soldiers, and then in the movie they had the "extra" limbs blown off to simulate what happens in battle.

Double Your Money

The man needed to send the money to his son. He knows, however, that letters are often intercepted and money is stolen. He posts all the left halves of the notes separately from all the right halves. When his son receives both envelopes, he sticks the banknotes together again.

Malfunction

He found a moth inside a prototype computer, which has led to the phrase "a computer bug."

A Friendly Match?

At Christmas in 1914 on the western front in World War I, the English and German soldiers fraternized and played a friendly game of football. Afterward, they went back to their trenches and to the war.

Lifesaver

The man was a hostage taken by kidnappers. Those who paid his ransom needed proof that he was still alive. He held a copy of the day's newspaper against his chest and was photographed to prove he was alive. Thereafter, the ransom was paid and the man was released.

The Plant

In a theater, two women were disputing the ownership of a very expensive coat. The police were called, and a policeman slipped the bag with talcum powder into a coat pocket and took it out in the presence of the two women. The impostor said, "That's not my coat!" But the real owner said, "I don't know how that got in there!"

Memory Transplant

The man kept forgetting his glasses, so he had laser eye surgery to improve his eyesight.

The Moggy's Ming

The man has an antique shop containing mostly junk, except for one very precious Ming bowl. He leaves it on the floor with some milk in it as the cat's feeding bowl. A typical dealer comes into the shop, sees all the useless rubbish, and is about to leave when he sees the precious bowl on the floor with the cat feeding from it. Reckoning that the owner is unaware of the bowl's value, he gets the bright idea of buying the cat for, say, $50, to which the owner reluctantly agrees. As he is leaving, he says, "Maybe the cat will be lonely without his little bowl. Will you throw it in for another $20?" "No," smiles the antique shop owner. "That is my lucky bowl. Why, I sell about twenty cats a week because of that little bowl!"

Stranger Danger

A baby boy was born in the house, but he lived for only a week. Naturally, his family mourned his passing away.

The Lethal Lie

The man was captured and being interrogated by the Mafia. He had stolen a huge amount of money from them and hidden it away. However, he did not speak their language, and they did not speak his, so they had to use an interpreter. Through the interpreter, they tell him that if he speaks the truth, he will not be killed. Then they tell him (all through the interpreter) that if he does not tell them where the money is, they will kill him. In fear, he tells the interpreter that the money is hidden at a certain address. The interpreter then says to the Mafia, "He won't tell you because he doesn't think you have the guts to kill him." So they take the man out and shoot him, and of course the interpreter later collects all the money.

Focus Pocus

The thief sprayed some pepper spray near the guard. The guard sneezed, and it is well known that you cannot sneeze with your eyes open. During these few seconds, the thief substituted a fake for the real jewel.

Outrage

The cartoon characters Fred and Wilma Flintstone were the first couple to appear in the same bed together on television.

First Time, Last Time

After having been convicted of murder, the dancer was being hanged. In the final moments of his hanging, the dancer's body, like many dying bodies, performed bizarre movements that novelist Henry Fielding called "the dance without music."

Speechless

Pierre was a criminal who was executed in France by guillotine. His severed head retained consciousness for a few seconds, during which time he could see his family but could not utter a sound.

Meeting and Greeting

The woman's hand had just been cut off in an accident, and she was hurrying to the hospital carrying it packed in ice in her handbag.

Playacting

The producer promised to put it on stage as part of a theatrical evening. He kept his promise by shredding the only copy of the script and using it as a snowstorm in another play.

The Uneaten

Nicholas, czar of Russia in the early 1900s, gave eggs made by Peter Fabergé as Easter presents for his children. The eggs were exquisitely made and became highly valued works of art.

Walk of Death

She was caught in a freak hailstorm and was bombarded with hailstones the size of tennis balls. The hailstones had all melted.

Defensive Measure

It was found that once an intruder had scaled a wall, he could not be seen breaking into the house or carrying out his crimes. A fence allowed people outside, whether neighbors or passers-by, to see an intruder and to raise the alarm.

Shaping the World

Mikhail Gorbachev, the former Russian leader, had a prominent birthmark on his head. When he found that a firm of vodka bottlers was using his name and face on their vodka bottles, he decided to copyright his name and the shape of his birthmark to prevent further misuse.

The Shot That Saved

The camera flash caused red-eye in the photo, but only in one eye. The other eye gave a white reflection. When the mother took the boy and the photo to a doctor, the boy was diagnosed with a cancerous tumor on the retina of one eye. This caused the white reflection. Red-eye is caused by the reflection from the capillaries in the back of a healthy eye. The boy's eye was operated on, the tumor removed, and his life was saved.

False Confession

When the man had been burgled the first time, he found the local police unresponsive. Several months later, when he saw two burglars in his garage, he called the police but was told no one was available. Exasperated, he called back and said, "Don't worry about those intruders. I shot them." Armed police arrived within minutes and arrested the burglars. The police complained, "I thought you said you shot them." He replied, "I thought you said no one was available."

Garment for Rent

The man was lost in a mine with many passages. He unraveled the sweater in order to leave a trail of thread that would allow him to trace his path out of the maze.

Key Decision

The man is trying to break into No. 10 Downing Street, the residence of the British Prime Minister. The key is fine, but for security reasons, No. 10 has a keyhole on the inside but not on the outside of the door.

A Long Way to Go for a Drink

The man wanted to smoke with his drink, and that was against the law in his country. Ireland made smoking illegal in public places in 2004. That's when many Irishmen began to travel to England in order to both smoke and drink.

Pop the Question

At their final dinner together, the woman ordered the least expensive item on the menu for each course. He deduced that if she had intended to accept his proposal of marriage, she would not have done this.

Custom and Practice

Twain said, "I use it as a nightcap!"

Towitt, Towoo

The forest was opposite a shopping center. In that shopping center was a shop that sold powerful binoculars. Customers who wanted to test the power of the binoculars could stand near the shop window and focus outside on the distant stuffed owl.

Plane Puzzler

The plane had just been picked up by another plane, a giant aircraft carrier, and so its engines could be safely switched off.

High Caliber

They were circus performers. The man was shot out of a cannon and landed in a net. One day, when he was ill, his wife took his place. Because she was lighter, she flew farther through the air, missed the net, and was killed on impact with the floor.

Wounded Enemy

This is classic military strategy. If you kill a soldier of the enemy, you reduce their forces by one. He just lies there, and the enemy may or may not bury him. But if you injure the enemy soldier so severely that he cannot fight again, he becomes a huge drain on the enemy's resources—men to rescue him and carry him off the battlefield, medical supplies, doctors, nurses, hospital supplies, rehabilitation, compensation, transport, psychological support, pension, etc.

Smoking Is Bad for You

The husband and wife had been threatened by a gangster. The couple had agreed to a code to signal danger. If the husband ever returned home and found his wife smoking a cigarette, he would know that danger was immediate. Furthermore, they agreed that she would point the cigarette in the direction of the danger. That way the husband knew that the gangster was hiding in the broom closet.

Determined to Die

The shot missed him but severed the rope. Jacques plunged into the sea, which put out the fire. He swallowed seawater, which made him vomit the poison. When he was washed up on shore, he was rescued but soon died of hypothermia. This reportedly happened on the coast of France, but it is probably an urban legend.

Hello, Grandma!

The office worker had taken off the previous day from work because, she claimed, she wanted to attend her only remaining grandmother's funeral.

Cake Killer

The woman was a diabetic. She checked her blood sugar level every day by pricking her finger to produce a little drop of blood, which she checked with a glucometer. However, since she had eaten a sugary cake with her fingers and had not washed her hands, quite an amount of sugar remained on her fingers. That sugar contaminated the tiny sample and gave a reading of sugar in her bloodstream way above what it actually was. The usual treatment for a high sugar reading is an immediate injection of insulin to use up the sugar (which, however, wasn't there!). This killed her.

Vacation, Vacation, Vacation

The bank analyzes trading patterns for any irregularities that might indicate fraud. If an employee, or trader, is absent for two weeks, that's enough time to allow the bank to discover any abnormal trading patterns he may have been involved in.

Clerical Advantage

According to medieval church custom, a bishop could have seven crosses on his tomb or gravestone, priests have five, and an ordinary person just one.

Bad Loser

The man was playing in a chess competition. After losing a game of chess to a computer, the man shot his opponent.

Puppy Love

In an exercise to build goodwill, a policeman brought a police dog into a local secondary school. The children were delighted to pet the dog. However, the dog had been trained to detect drugs, and it correctly identified six children who were carrying marijuana.

Death at the Door

When driving, the woman fell asleep at the wheel of her car and plunged into a canal. Inside the car at the bottom of the canal, she called 911. The emergency operator advised her to roll down the window and swim to safety, but water had ruined the electrical motor that operated the window, so it would not open. She tried to open the door but could not because the pressure of the water was too great. Eventually, the water flowed into the car and she drowned.

The Lethal Warning

The men were skiing. When one man called out to warn his friend about the risks of an avalanche, his loud shout caused the very thing he feared.

Field of Gold

A farmer sprayed his field with golden dye because it was featured in a film about the life of Vincent van Gogh. One of van Gogh's famous paintings features a golden wheat field.

Good Bump

She had forgotten to close the trunk. As she bumped violently over the speed bump the trunk lid clicked closed.

Timeless

The Virgin Mary has appeared more often on Time magazine than any other woman.

Chilly

The coldest desert on earth is in Antarctica. The whole continent is a desert because there is virtually no precipitation there.

The Silly Salesman

As he drove along the Florida freeway at 80 mph (about 130 kph) to reach his appointment, the salesman read his sales manual. Not surprisingly, he crashed the car and was killed.

This 1993 event won a Darwin Award (for stupidity).

It's Not True!

It was an English class. The teacher showed how punctuation can change the meaning of the sentence. First she wrote, "Woman without her man is helpless." Then she wrote, "Woman! Without her, man is helpless."

Not Here, Son

The schoolboy was an avid hurdler. The only hurdles he could find were gravestones in the church cemetery. So he practiced there. The police stopped him from this irreverent behavior.

Unsanitary Janitor

At a school for teenage girls, there had been a problem. The girls applied lipstick and then kissed the mirror on the bathroom wall to check to see if their lipstick was applied evenly. The headmistress called in all the girls and showed them how the caretaker cleaned the mirror. He deliberately dipped his mop in the toilet first. From then on, none of the girls kissed the mirror.

Hyper-Inflation

The bottle was signed by all four members of the Beatles and immediately became valuable as a collector's item the night John Lennon died.

WALLY Test I Answers

1. Young men.

2. KEY. It completes the word *donkey*, and a key starts a car.

3. The other half.

4. As fur as you can.

5. Just above the Pair O'Shins.

6. Dwight D. Eiffel Tower.

7. It quacks up.

8. Whenever he goes to work he gets the sack!

9. The ultrasound department.

WALLY Test I is on p. 29.

WALLY Test II Answers

1. He does it during the daytime.

2. If you don't know where you are going, why are you standing in line?

3. V, W, X, Y, and Z.

4. Consider the facts: One hundred rats would kill a cat.

5. Water.

6. It is a mail bag.

7. Wet rocks.

8. October is the longest month. It has 31 days, and it gains an extra hour when the clocks are turned back.

9. In the center of the ship where the funnel be.

WALLY Test II is on p. 68.

INDEX

answers, 69–90

Bad Bump, 14
  clues, 51
  solution, 71
Bad Loser, 43
  clues, 65
  solution, 87
Birds of a Feather, 24
  clues, 56
  solution, 77

Cake Killer, 41
  clues, 64
  solution, 87
Cheaper by the Dozen, 21
  clues, 55
  solution, 75
Chilly, 46
  clues, 66
  solution, 89
Clerical Advantage, 42
  clues, 65
  solution, 87
Clever Detective, 14
  clues, 51
  solution, 71
clues, 49–67
Custom and Practice, 38
  clues, 62
  solution, 84

Deadly Delivery, 24
  clues, 56
  solution, 77
Deadly Talk, 16
  clues, 52
  solution, 72
Death at the Door, 44
  clues, 65
  solution, 88
Death by Reading, 19
  clues, 53
  solution, 74
Defensive Measure, 34
  clues, 61
  solution, 82

Determined to Die, 40
  clues, 64
  solution, 86
Difference in Attitude, 15
  clues, 51
  solution, 72
Double Your Money, 25
  clues, 57
  solution, 78
Drink and Die I and II, 13
  clues, 50
  solutions, 70

Elementary, 20
  clues, 54
  solution, 74

False Confession, 35
  clues, 61
  solution, 83
Fatal Fork, 24
  clues, 56
  solution, 77
Field of Gold, 45
  clues, 66
  solution, 88
First Time, Last Time, 31
  clues, 59
  solution, 81
Focus Pocus, 30
  clues, 59
  solution, 80
A Friendly Match?, 26
  clues, 57
  solution, 78
Fruit of Sarcasm, 17
  clues, 52
  solution, 73

Garment for Rent, 36
  clues, 61
  solution, 83
Good Bump, 45
  clues, 66
  solution, 88
Groovy Movie, 25
  clues, 57
  solution, 77

Hello, Grandma!, 41
  clues, 64
  solution, 86
High Caliber, 39
  clues, 63
  solution, 85
High Flyer, 23
  clues, 56
  solution, 76
Hyper-Inflation, 47
  clues, 67
  solution, 90

Insecure, 16
  clues, 52
  solution, 72
It's Not True! 46
  clues, 67
  solution, 89

Key Decision, 36
  clues, 62
  solution, 84

Lakeless, 22
  clues, 55
  solution, 76
lateral thinking,
  defined, 9
Lethal Lie, 30
  clues, 59
  solution, 80
Lethal Warning, 44
  clues, 66
  solution, 88
Lifesaver, 27
  clues, 57
  solution, 79
Long Way to Go for a
  Drink, 37
  clues, 62
  solution, 84

Malfunction, 26
  clues, 57
  solution, 78

Meeting and Greeting, 32
    clues, 60
    solution, 81
Memory Transplant, 27
    clues, 58
    solution, 79
Moggy's Ming, 28
    clues, 58
    solution, 79
My Condiments to the
    Chef, 19
    clues, 53
    solution, 74

No Claims Bonus, 18
    clues, 53
    solution, 73
Not Here, Son, 47
    clues, 67
    solution, 89

Only in the U.S.A., 21
    clues, 54
    solution, 75
Oskar, 12
    clues, 50
    solution, 70
Outrage, 31
    clues, 59
    solution, 80

Picture Book, 22
    clues, 55
    solution, 76
Plane Puzzler, 39
    clues, 63
    solution, 85
Plant, The, 27
    clues, 58
    solution, 79
Playacting, 33
    clues, 60
    solution, 81

Poor Pet, 23
    clues, 56
    solution, 76
Pop the Question, 37
    clues, 62
    solution, 84
Puppy Love, 43
    clues, 65
    solution, 88
puzzles, 11–48

Quarters, 12
    clues, 50
    solution, 70

Racing Certainty, 17
    clues, 52
    solution, 73
Red-Faced, 22
    clues, 55
    solution, 76

Second of One, 18
    clues, 53
    solution, 74
Shaping the World, 35
    clues, 61
    solution, 82
Shot That Saved, The, 35
    clues, 61
    solution, 82
Silent Robber, 15
    clues, 51
    solution, 72
Silly Salesman, 46
    clues, 67
    solution, 89
Smoking Is Bad for You,
    40
    clues, 64
    solution, 85
Speechless, 32
    clues, 59

solution, 81
Stranger Danger, 28
    clues, 58
    solution, 80

Taking the Right Steps, 20
    clues, 54
    solution, 74
Timeless, 45
    clues, 66
    solution, 89
Timepiece, 17
    clues, 52
    solution, 73
Towitt, Towoo, 38
    clues, 63
    solution, 84
Traffic Offense, 14
    clues, 50
    solution, 71

Uneaten, The, 33
    clues, 60
    solution, 81
Unsanitary Janitor, 47
    clues, 67
    solution, 90

Vacation, Vacation,
    Vacation, 42
    clues, 64
    solution, 87

Walk of Death, 34
    clues, 60
    solution, 82
WALLY Test I, 29
    answers, 91
WALLY Test II, 68
    answers, 92
Wounded Enemy, 39
    clues, 63
    solution, 85

About the Authors

Paul Sloane lives in Camberley, Surrey, England. He has been an avid collector and composer of lateral thinking puzzles for many years. He runs the Lateral Puzzles Forum on the Internet, where you can set and solve puzzles interactively: **www.lateralpuzzles.com**

Mr. Sloane has his own business helping organizations use lateral thinking to find creative solutions and improve innovation. The Web site is: **www.destination-innovation.com**

He is a renowned speaker and course leader. He is married with three daughters, and in his spare time he plays golf, chess, tennis, and keyboards in an aging rock band, the Fat Cats.

Des MacHale was born in County Mayo, Ireland. He lives in Cork with his wife Anne and their five children. He's an associate professor of mathematics at University College Cork. He has a passionate interest in puzzles of all sorts and has written over 60 books on various subjects—lateral thinking puzzles, jokes, a biography of the mathematician George Boole, insights on John Ford's film *The Quiet Man*, and a nine-volume *Wit* series of humorous quotations. He has published puzzles in the Brainteaser section of *The Sunday Times* of London.

Mr. MacHale's other interests include bird-watching (ah, so relaxing), classical music and Irish traditional music, book collecting, photography, old movies, tennis, quizzes, words, humor, broadcasting, and health education. In fact, he's interested in everything except wine, jazz, and Demi Moore. (Our apologies to Ms. Moore.)

Paul Sloane and Des MacHale are the authors of ten lateral-thinking puzzle books for Sterling Publishing Co., Inc. More recent titles include *Classic Lateral Thinking Challenges, Challenging Lateral Thinking Puzzles, Colorful Lateral Thinking Puzzles, Great Lateral Thinking Puzzles, Improve Your Lateral Thinking, Intriguing Lateral Thinking Puzzles,* and *Brain-Busting Lateral Thinking Puzzles.*